Introduction

Demonism is neither funny nor phony.

It is real. It is, in fact, as serious and significant a subject as can ever be considered. But, strangely, it remains one of those unmentionables. Almost like, "Let's not talk about it and maybe it will go away." We Christians avoid it like the plague. And when we do discuss it, our comments fall somewhere between traditional superstition and downright ignorance.

Even though we have ignored it, the world has explored it. By twisting the truth and pushing the hot buttons of human curiosity and gross sensuality, slick promoters have turned it into a money-making extravaganza . . . a weird sideshow attraction with all the crowd-pleasing gimmicks. *And the devil could not be happier.* The last thing he wants is to have his presence and his strategy exposed.

Although brief, this booklet is an attempt to draw back the thick veil of fear and uncertainty about our adversary. Christians need to be informed of the truth—that we *have* the victory, that we are more than conquerors rather than helpless victims when it comes to dealing with Satan and his demons. If you are interested in what God has promised, what protection you possess, and what techniques you can use with confidence, this booklet is for you.

Charles R. Swindoll

Demonism

The church of Jesus Christ lost a gallant warrior of the faith with the recent passing of Merrill F. Unger. It was my choice privilege to study Hebrew under this fine Semitic scholar during my years in seminary. He may be gone in body, but certainly not in memory. Anyone who sat under Dr. Unger's teaching will never forget his devotion to the Lord Jesus Christ, which was revealed in his unique prayers before every class session and his dedication to the truth of Scripture.

Of special interest to Dr. Unger throughout his ministry was the subject of demonism. Although he has gone home to be with the Lord he loved so dearly, his zeal and insights have been preserved in several books on that subject which he left in his legacy. One I would heartily recommend is entitled *Demons in the World Today*. In that volume these words appear:

> *Certainly there is no excuse for the church to surrender its charismatic power to heal and deliver from satanic oppression. In the very measure that it does, it advertises its spiritual*

> *bankruptcy and makes itself a weak institution that no longer commands the respect of the spiritually needy masses. No wonder multitudes are seeking spiritual reality in Oriental religions, non-Christian faiths, and occult-oriented perversions of Christianity. Christian faith is so devitalized by apostasy and so contaminated with men's opinions and a defective presentation of Jesus Christ that it is becoming a hollow shell, powerless to affect men's lives.*[1]

I could not agree more completely. Long enough have Christians taken a tongue-in-cheek approach to the issue of demonism! It is time for us to stand up, stand firm, and stand against the powers of darkness in the strength of our Lord Jesus Christ. Boldly and confidently, we have every right to deny the adversary *any* ground he attempts to claim by means of trickery and intimidation.

Ignorance Must Be Dispelled

There appears in 2 Corinthians 2:11 a short but powerful statement concerning the devil.

> *in order that no advantage be taken of us by Satan; for we are not ignorant of his schemes.*

The writer's concern is that the Corinthian believers fully and completely forgive an individual in their local church. They are told to reaffirm their love for him (v. 8) and to prove their obedience (v. 9) by not restraining themselves in this act of forgiveness.

Why? So Satan would not be able to take advantage of that situation. In other words, their sustained *lack* of forgiveness would give the enemy an opportunity to wedge his way into their fellowship and accomplish his insidious objectives. Their disobedience could become the adversary's ground of entrance. He patiently awaits such open doors and cleverly makes his moves at such times.

But what does Paul declare? He says, "We are not ignorant of his schemes." In effect, he is saying, "We know his style. We are constantly aware of his methods and strategy. He doesn't have us fooled!" Strong, confident, reassuring words. But are they true of *you*? Paul could say that, but can *you*?

Before any opponent can be intelligently withstood, a knowledge of his ways must be known. Ignorance must be dispelled. No boxer in his right mind enters the ring without having first studied the other boxer's style. The same is true on the football field. Or the battlefield. Days (some times *months*) are spent studying the tactics, the weaknesses, the strengths of the opponent. Ignorance is an enemy to victory.

I urge you to make a serious study—on your own, from the Bible—of the devil and his host of demons. This little booklet cannot do that for you, but it can be a source of motivation. Remember, ignorance of the enemy puts you at his mercy and steals from you the confidence you need to stand against his strategy. *Inform yourself!*

Armor Must Be Worn

Turn next in your Bible to Ephesians 6:10-14. These five verses will prove to be very helpful in your understanding of the battle that is going on. I would suggest that you memorize them during the next several days.

> *Finally, be strong in the Lord, and in the strength of His might.*
>
> *Put on the full armor of God, that you may be able to stand firm against the schemes of the devil.*
>
> *For our struggle is not against flesh and blood, but against the rulers, against the powers, against the world forces of this darkness, against the spiritual forces of wickedness in the heavenly places.*
>
> *Therefore, take up the full armor of God, that you may be able to resist in the evil day, and having done everything, to stand firm.*
>
> *Stand firm therefore, ...*

A close look will reveal four two-word commands. Get a pencil and underscore each one.

Verse 10	Be strong!
Verse 11	Put on!
Verse 13	Take up!
Verse 14	Stand firm!

Let's spend a few minutes thinking about each one before we move on to the actual strategies we can employ against demonic attacks.

Be Strong!

Because the battle is an invisible warfare, our strength is not external. This refers to inner strength, as the tenth verse concludes, ". . . in the strength of His might," referring to the Lord Jesus Christ. We are to be strong in Him. Lean on Him, by faith. Turn to Him in prayer. Walk with Him in confident trust . . . drawing upon *His* power.

Why? This is best answered in another section of the New Testament.

> *And when you were dead in your transgressions and the uncircumcision of your flesh, He made you alive together with Him, having forgiven us all our transgressions, having cancelled out the certificate of debt consisting of decrees against us and which was hostile to us; and He has taken it out of the way, having nailed it to the cross. When He had disarmed the rulers and authorities, He made a public display of them, having triumphed over them through Him* (Colossians 2:13-15).

At the cross, when Christ Jesus died, He "disarmed" all creatures of darkness. He "triumphed over them." So then, He is the champion. When you turn to Him for strength, you are turning to the One who has sovereign authority over them. He won it at the cross. Be strong in the strength of the Champion.

Put On!

Put on what? Ephesians 6:11 spells it out. We are to wear "the full armor of God" so we may be able to stand firm against the enemy's schemes. Good troops who fight well are well-equipped. Inferior weapons and poor equipment spell sure defeat.

Each piece of the armor is explained in Ephesians 6:14-17 (read verses 14 through 17 slowly and carefully), and each one is extremely important. The armor is designed to protect you *and* give you confidence in battle. Now I warn you, when you realize that this battle is unlike any other, it is easy to become fearful, intimidated, and shy. When you realize you cannot actually see the enemy but he can see you, you are naturally seized with panic.

All the more reason to put on the armor God has provided. Put it on, Christian.

Take Up!

It is there, available and waiting, to be claimed. The full supply is yours—tailor-made to fit your personality, your set of circumstances, and your need. Reach out by faith and mentally "take up" the armor of God. You'll learn how to use it in days to come; but first, grab hold of it.

The day after I joined the Marines, I found myself in a room full of green, raw, frightened recruits. We were issued a seabag full of clothing plus a rifle, a cartridge belt, a bayonet, and a heavy steel helmet. We were also provided with a "bucket issue" . . . the basic supplies for our hygienic needs (the Corps had another name for it!). There we stood, scared and ignorant. Lowly privates not at all aware of what was ahead of us. Within the next thirteen weeks we would discover how to wear and use everything . . . but for the time being, we were given one loud command: *"Pick it up!"* That's what God says to you today.

Stand Firm!

This is so important, the same words appear three separate times (Ephesians 6:11, 13, 14).

These are the words of confidence and assurance. They tell us we have nothing to be afraid of. Nothing. After all, the One who does the fighting for us is the Champion. And the enemy is already defeated—it happened at the cross, remember? Of course, he doesn't want you to know that. Which explains why his favorite strategy is deception. He will throw up smoke screens that may appear terrifying and scary and awfully impressive . . . but behind all that noise and smoke is a full awareness that he is defeated.

So whatever you do in dealing with demons, Christian, do it with confidence. With absolute, victorious assurance. He is the victim; you are the victor. So stand firm!

Resisting the Enemy

In the thirteenth verse of this same section of Scripture (Ephesians 6), we are told the purpose of our putting on the armor and standing firm.

> . . . *that you may be able to resist in the evil day*. . . .

Such days will come.

Some of you who read my words are very much aware of "the evil day." You have been harrassed and attacked and badgered by the enemy. Either against yourself or someone else . . . or both. Others of you are inexperienced and can only imagine what is involved in demonic oppression. Take it from me, it is horrible. It is ugly. It is vile. It is like nothing else you will ever encounter. It is exhausting and relentless. It is "evil," as the verse states. He may be a defeated foe, but he won't give up without a struggle.

Explanation of Demonic Involvement

We first need to understand the desire of our adversary. He wants, more than anything else, to have his way in the lives of humans. He wants to control us, or at least to win a hearing and become a persuasive force in our lives. His preferred realm of operation is our *minds*. This is seen in the following two verses of Scripture.

> *For though we walk in the flesh, we do not war according to the flesh, for the weapons of our warfare are not of the flesh, but divinely powerful for the destruction of fortresses. We are destroying speculations and every lofty thing raised up against the knowledge of God, and we are taking every thought captive to the obedience of Christ* (2 Corinthians 10:3-5).
>
> *But I am afraid, lest as the serpent deceived Eve by his craftiness, your minds should be led astray from the simplicity and purity of devotion to Christ* (2 Corinthians 11:3).

Yes, that's it. "Led astray" says it best. It is the idea of getting us off course, sidetracked, pulled off target. Ultimately, his hope is to gain full control.

And because demons exist in spirit form (they have no physical bodies), they possess a strong desire to operate within a body, ideally a *human* body. All the more reason to "stand firm" against their strategy.

During our Lord's earthly ministry He encountered demonized people on several occasions. By the way, demon "possession" and demon "oppression" are not actual biblical terms. The Greek text supports only the idea of one being "demonized," which may include any one of several levels of demonic activity and/or control. Sometimes the involvement was so deep that demons had to be expelled or exorcised from individuals. On other occasions, the person under attack was told to "resist." Resisting the enemy is mentioned in the Ephesians 6 passage we just looked at as well as James 4:7.

Submit therefore to God. Resist the devil and he will flee from you.

This is a very practical instruction. No hocus pocus. No repeating of the same word or phrase over and over again. No secret code or religious "mantra." Resisting means *resisting.* Shoving away. Pushing aside. Not allowing to stay or enter.

Suggestions for Resisting the Devil

Maybe a simple process to follow will help.

1. Vocally declare your faith in the Lord Jesus Christ. Use His full title as you do this. Openly acknowledge that He is your Master, your Lord, and the One who has conquered all other powers at the cross.

2. Deny any and all allegiance to the devil, his demonic host, and the occult. Do this forcefully and boldly. Again, express these things aloud.

3. Claim the full armor of God, based on Ephesians 6:10-17 as your complete protection. Read the passage orally with emphasis.

4. Finally, state firmly your resistance of demonic influence.

Consider using the following "Prayer of Resistance." Use it as a guide when you begin to feel afraid and sense the attack of evil forces.

I do now renounce any and all allegiance I have ever given to Satan and his host of wicked spirits. I refuse to be influenced or intimidated by them. And I refuse to be used by them in any way whatsoever. I reject all their attacks upon my body, my spirit, my soul, and my mind. I claim the shed blood of the Lord Jesus Christ throughout my being. And I revoke all their power and influence within me or round about me. I resist them in the name of my Lord and Master, Jesus Christ, the Champion over evil. I stand secure in the power of the cross of Calvary whereby Satan and all his powers became defeated foes through the blood of my Lord Jesus Christ. I stand upon the promises of God's Word. In humble faith, I do here and now put on the whole armor of God that enables me to stand firm against the schemes of the devil.

While these words are certainly not "inspired," they may prove very helpful as you stand firm against the wicked one.

And one more thought about resisting: Claim the promise of James 4:7. Speaking of satanic opposition,

. . . he will flee from you.

Stand on that hope. Refuse the temptation to doubt the reality of God's promise to you. The enemy is defeated. He runs when you call his bluff. The blood of the cross carries with it divine clout. Fall back upon the transaction that occurred at the cross—Christ's blood for your sins.

Casting Out Demons

There are occasions when the demon(s) have become so entrenched within a life that the need to cast them out is evident. This is a much more emotional, wrenching experience and it calls for help from other Christians. Scripture suggests that resisting is something one does on his own, but when demons were actually expelled in biblical days, others were involved to assist in the process.

A Biblical Case Study

Several times in the Gospels and Acts we read of demons being exorcised. The example I'd like to refer to briefly is in Luke 8:26-33.

> *And they sailed to the country of the Gerasenes, which is opposite Galilee.*
>
> *And when He had come out onto the land, He was met by a certain man from the city who was possessed with demons; and who had not put on any clothing for a long time, and was not living in a house, but in the tombs.*
>
> *And seeing Jesus, he cried out and fell before Him, and said in a loud voice, "What do I have to do with You, Jesus, Son of the Most High God? I beg You, do not torment me."*
>
> *For He had been commanding the unclean spirit to come out of the man. For it had seized him many times; and he was bound with chains and shackles*

> *and kept under guard; and yet he would burst his fetters and be driven by the demon into the desert.*
>
> *And Jesus asked him, "What is your name?" And he said, "Legion"; for many demons had entered him.*
>
> *And they were entreating Him not to command them to depart into the abyss.*
>
> *Now there was a herd of many swine feeding there on the mountain; and the demons entreated Him to permit them to enter the swine. And He gave them permission.*
>
> *And the demons came out from the man and entered the swine; and the herd rushed down the steep bank into the lake, and were drowned.*

The man Jesus met was demonized ("possess" is not in the Greek text in verse 27). Within the man's person was the actual presence of evil forces—"many demons" (v. 30)—whose spokesman was named *Legion*. No need to repeat all the details of the man's demeanor, but obviously he bore the marks of torment. And he had incredible strength. He must have been a frightful sight.

Calmly and yet firmly our Lord spoke to the demons within and, using the man's vocal cords, answers were given by Legion. Interestingly, the demons did not want to return to "the abyss," apparently a place of permanent removal, so Jesus allowed these demons to enter into a nearby herd of swine, which they did, and subsequently the swine were drowned.

The man, now relieved of those tormenting spirits, is suddenly a changed individual. Look at the difference in verse 35:

> *And the people went out to see what had happened; and they came to Jesus, and found the man from whom the demons had gone out, sitting down at the feet of Jesus, clothed and in his right mind; and they became frightened.*

Clothed and in his right mind, the man was wonderfully delivered by the power of the Son of God.

I mentioned earlier that the man had been "demonized." Perhaps it is advisable for me to amplify this a bit. Unless we understand what the presence of a demon (or demons) can do in a life, we'll lack the necessary compassion to assist those in desperate need.

An Explanation of Being "Demonized"

When one or more demons inhabit the body of an individual, that person finds himself under the control of the evil spirit(s). By temporarily blotting out his consciousness, the demon can speak and act through the victim, using him as his slave or tool. During such times (as we saw in Luke 8), the person often possesses incredible strength, a blasphemous, vile, vulgar tongue, a wild, violent temperament that goes to unbelievable extremes, and frequently carries out dangerous actions against himself and others. It is not uncommon for the demonized victim to be driven to the most sadistic, brutal, and perverted forms of attack on others . . . to the ultimate extreme of murder.

It has been my observation that when a demon speaks and projects itself through its victim, the voice is different from the person's normal voice and personality. I have seen times when the evil spirit who speaks uses another language, totally unfamiliar to the victim. It is also interesting that the pronouns being used help you identify the presence of an alien being. The *first* person pronoun ("I" and "me") consistently designates the inhabiting demon. Bystanders are addressed in the *second* person ("you" or "your"). The demonized victim is referred to in the *third* person ("him," "her," or "his") and is looked upon during the attack as unconscious and for all practical purposes as nonexistent during this interval.

You will recall that the man in Luke 8 is virtually a passive "vehicle" used to carry about in his body the evil spirits. Naked, ferocious, and possessing superhuman strength, he was "driven by the demon" (v. 29). A very pathetic, descriptive scene. But after the demons were expelled, Dr. Luke informs us that the man was quiet, clothed, and completely under control (v. 35). The anguish and inner pressures were gone. In fact, if you read on in the Luke 8 account, you'll see that the man wanted to accompany the Lord Jesus Christ. When told by the Savior not to do so but rather go back home and announce what great things God had done for him, he gladly obeyed. There was a *remarkable and sudden contrast* that swept over the man once the demons were gone.

I have witnessed this on several occasions. Torment is replaced with a calm, quiet response. Ugly and profane remarks are stopped and replaced with praise and gratitude to God. It is beautiful to behold!

A Necessary Warning to All

Bold confrontation is often needed. When people have become demonized, they need help . . . immediate, courageous, compassionate help. But let me warn you, spiritual warfare is no trifling matter! And lest you allow idle curiosity to draw you into the idea that such a ministry would be fun 'n games, *please proceed with caution.* No one becomes an "expert" in a deliverance ministry. Our only ground of victory over evil powers is our union with the Lord Jesus Christ. The spirits of darkness are unpredictable, extremely crafty, and ever so brilliant.

I draw upon the writing of Mark Bubeck for some dos and don'ts which will prove helpful. I've summarized what he has explained in greater detail in a book I heartily recommend, written by this capable author.

Here are the "Don'ts":[2]

• *Don't* seek information or allow any wicked spirit to volunteer information you do not seek.

• *Don't* believe what a wicked spirit says unless you test it. They are inevitable liars like their leader Satan.

• *Don't* be afraid of their threatening of harm to you or your family.

• *Don't* assume that one victory is the end of the warfare.

• *Don't* rely upon bold confrontation as the main way to victory over the enemy. The positive application of doctrine, warfare praying, scripture memorization, and a walk of praise toward God are very essential.

And now some "Do's":[3]

• *Do* daily put on the whole armor of God and claim your union with Christ and walk in the fulness of the Holy Spirit.

• *Do* take back all ground you may have given Satan by careless, willful sins of the flesh. A simple prayer of faith accomplishes this.

• *Do* bind all powers of darkness, commanding all of them to leave when he does.

• *Do* force the wicked spirit to admit that because you are seated with Christ far above all principalities and powers (Ephesians 1:21; 2:6) that you have full authority over them.

• *Do* force them to admit that when you command them to leave that they have to go where Christ sends them.

• *Do* demand that if the wicked power has divided into several parts, that he become a whole spirit.

• *Do* be prepared for the wicked power to try to hurt the person you are working with in some manner. Sudden body pains, a severe headache, a choking experience, and the like, are very often used.

Can a Christian Be Demonized?

For a number of years I questioned this, but I am now convinced it can occur. If a "ground of entrance" has been granted the power of darkness (such as trafficking in the occult, a continual unforgiving spirit, a habitual state of carnality, etc.), the demon(s) sees this as a green light —okay to proceed (2 Corinthians 2:10-11; 1 Corinthians 5:1-5; Luke 22:31-32). Wicked forces are not discriminating with regard to which body they may inhabit. I have worked personally with troubled, anguished Christians for many years. On a few occasions I have assisted in the painful process of relieving them of demons.

Perhaps a clarifying word of assurance is needed here. The believer *has* the Holy Spirit resident within. Therefore, the alien, wicked spirit certainly cannot claim "ownership" of the Christian. He is *still* a child of God. But while present within the body (perhaps in the region of the soul) that evil force can work havoc within the life, bringing the most extreme thoughts imaginable into his or her conscious awareness. Couldn't this explain how some believers can fall into such horrible sins? And how some could commit suicide?

Demon Confrontation Today

How does all this relate to us today? Well, there are several factors that apply to us. I have three in mind.

1. *There must be a correct diagnosis.* We need to guard against witch-hunting. Some people see demons in most every area of weakness or wrong. I've even heard of one man who believed a person he knew had "the demon of nail-biting." No, I doubt that biting one's fingernails is prompted by demons. Furthermore, there are characteristics among the mentally and emotionally disturbed that are bizarre . . . but not necessarily demonic. And there can be physical disorders as well. All of this tells us we must be very careful and discerning when it comes to diagnosis.

Some of the things to look for that might reveal demonism, however, are:

- Sudden and unreasonable changes of moods
- Aggressive, unrestrainable expressions of hostility
- Unnatural attachment to charms, fortune-telling, and involvement in the occult
- Extreme, enslaving habits of sexual immorality, perversions, gross blasphemy, and unashamed mockery.

All these and other characteristics need to be observed with a discerning eye. Counsel with others is of great help at this point. Be cautious about making a premature diagnosis.

2. *There must be help provided the demonized person.* If you become convinced that demons are, in fact, involved, the demonized person will need assistance from caring, strong Christians who will work together in relieving the victim of evil. A careful study of Jesus' procedure is urged. For example, He sought the name of the demon. He took charge and did not relinquish control. He also commanded that the demon come out. *It is never advisable that this process be attempted alone.* There is strength in numbers . . . especially mature, discerning Christians. Such experiences can be extremely difficult and violent.

3. *There must be follow-up support after the ordeal.* A most vulnerable time occurs after the individual is relieved of demonism. A great deal of care and support is needed. Glance over Luke 11:24-26. It will help you see the value of follow-up.

> *"When the unclean spirit goes out of a man, it passes through waterless places seeking rest, and not finding any, it*

says, 'I will return to my house from which I came.'

"And when it comes, it finds it swept and put in order.

"Then it goes and takes along seven other spirits more evil than itself, and they go in and live there; and the last state of that man becomes worse than the first."

Do not leave the individual without your assistance.

Summary and Conclusion

We have covered a lot of territory in these few pages. We have discovered that in order for us to stand our ground and do battle victoriously against the powers of darkness, ignorance must be dispelled and the armor God has provided must be taken up and put on. We also determined that there are two basic ways the Bible teaches us to deal with demons: (1) to resist them, and (2) to cast them out. These truths have helped us realize that in Jesus Christ we are the victors, the conquerors. There is no need to be afraid. We have overcoming power through Him who died that we might live. Stand firm, Christian. Through Christ we conquer.

I can think of no more appropriate way to conclude these thoughts than to quote Revelation 12:11, a verse that says it all about our spiritual war with Satan.

"And they overcame him because of the blood of the Lamb and because of the word of their testimony, and they did not love their life even to death."

Almighty God and faithful Friend:

You know the times in which we live are wicked, perverse, and increasingly more godless as every year passes. And it is so easy for us to become frightened, since we are surrounded by every evidence of gross evil. As your children we are like an island of purity surrounded by a troubled dark sea of depravity . . . a place where satanic and demonic activity is happening.

And on top of all that, we cannot see our real enemy. Therefore, we cannot reach out and fight him with our fists. But he is there, relentlessly and ruthlessly working against You and Your will. This frightens us, we freely admit. But we have learned that there is no reason to be afraid. Your armor is all we need. Your strength is our shield.

Convince us of this, O Lord. Reassure us that You are our light, our protection, and our shield. We need those reminders. Give them to us each day. May we stand firm in Your power as we find our confidence in You rather than tremble before the enemy. Only through the blood of our Lord Jesus Christ do we conquer!

We pray in the strong name of Your Son. Amen.

¹Merrill F. Unger, *Demons in the World Today* (Wheaton, Illinois: Tyndale House Publishers, 1971), p. 190.

²Mark I. Bubeck, *The Adversary* (Chicago: Moody Press, 1975), p. 124. Used by permission of Moody Bible Institute.

³Ibid., p. 125.